A *Bird*
WATCHING

A *Bird* WATCHING

Poems

VICTORIA WYTTENBERG

MoonPath Press

Poetry
ISBN 978-1-936657-76-6

Cover art: collage, after Gabrielle Munter,
by Victoria Wyttenberg

Author painting by June Weisman

Book design by Tonya Namura, using Guess Pro (display) and
Garamond Premier Pro (text).

MoonPath Press, an imprint of Concrete Wolf Poetry Series,
is dedicated to publishing the finest poets living
in the U.S. Pacific Northwest.

MoonPath Press
PO Box 445
Tillamook, OR 97141

MoonPathPress@gmail.com

http://MoonPathPress.com

For those I love who have died:
my mother, father, sister, brother, husband, daughter, son.

ACKNOWLEDGMENTS

Thank you to the editors and the journals in which these poems appeared:

The Bellwether Review: "Potatoes"

Clackamas Literary Review: "My Brother Enters Enchantment"

Hubbub: "Mother in Heaven"

Malahat Review: "For My Oldest Child," "Tulips"

Poetry Canada: "Flowers Have Beauty and Roots Have Worth"

Poetry Northwest: "The Boy With Two Frogs," "The Curse," "The School Photographer," "The Sea Lion," "To Change Shape"

Portland Review: "Astigmatism"

The Red Door: "Pomegranate"

Rock Creek Review: "Potatoes," "Sunflowers"

Seattle Review: "Blue Heron"

Willow Springs: "Leaves Going to Yellow," "Letter From My Father Somewhere in the South Pacific, 1944"

"The School Photographer" also appeared in *From Here We Speak: An Anthology of Oregon Poetry*.

"Blue Heron," "Flowers Have Beauty and Roots Have Worth," "For My Oldest Child," and "The School Photographer" also appeared in *Millennial Spring: Eight New Oregon Poets*, edited by Peter Sears and Michael Malan.

"The Curse" also appeared in *Northwest Poetry Anthology*.

"Blue Heron" also appeared in *Portland Lights: A Poetry Anthology*, edited by Barbara La Morticella and Steve Nemiow.

"Blue Heron" also appeared in *Walking Bridges: Using Poetry as a Compass*.

"Blue Heron" and "Invisible Choir" also appeared in *What the River Brings: Oregon River Poems*.

GRATITUDE

Thank you and deep gratitude to all my teachers, especially David Biespiel, Matthew Dickman, and Christopher Howell.

Thank you to Lana Hechtman Ayers and MoonPath Press for publishing this book.

These are the days when Birds come back—
A very few–a Bird or two–
To take a backward look.
—Emily Dickinson

There is special providence in the fall of a sparrow.
—William Shakespeare, *Hamlet*

And the memory of everything we have loved remains
and returns in the evening of our life. It is not dead,
but asleep, and it is good to collect a great store of it.
—Vincent van Gogh, letter to his brother Theo
dated May 30,1877

CONTENTS

ACKNOWLEDGMENTS   vii

GRATITUDE   ix

BOY WITH TWO FROGS   3

FLOWERS HAVE BEAUTY AND ROOTS
     HAVE WORTH   4

SUNFLOWERS   6

THE SEA LION   7

ASTIGMATISM   9

THE SCHOOL PHOTOGRAPHER   10

MOTHER IN HEAVEN   12

POMEGRANATE   13

FOR MY OLDEST CHILD   14

MY BROTHER ENTERS ENCHANTMENT   16

ASHES TO ASHES   18

LETTER FROM MY FATHER SOMEWHERE
     IN THE SOUTH PACIFIC, 1944   20

POTATOES   22

LEAVES GOING TO YELLOW   24

CURSE FOR AN EX HUSBAND   26

COAT   27

THE HEART HOLDS OUT EMPTY HANDS   29

LET YOURSELF CHANGE SHAPE   30

TRYING TO CHANGE MY LIFE WITH
     CANARD À L'ORANGE   32

TULIPS   34

SEPTEMBER, ROGUE RIVER   35

BEGONIA   37

DRAGONFLIES   39

WATER, CUP, SPOON, HOUSE   40

CROW   43

FISH IN THE BLOOD AND
  A BIRD WATCHING   45

THE BURIAL OF CASAGEMAS   47

BLUE HERON   49

TURNING THE BONES   50

INVISIBLE CHOIR   52

PEONY   53

ABOUT THE AUTHOR   55

A *Bird* WATCHING

BOY WITH TWO FROGS

A boy holds a frog in each hand
and is truly happy. He holds the frogs gently,
and they talk to him, their eyes topaz.
He believes stories and imagines
the thighs of the princess. His eyes
find odd faces, bumpy skin like gourds,
throbbing song.

He loves their smell like wet balloons,
breathes in the music of their croaks,
and dreams his own voice among cowslips,
filling the night air one leap from water.
Twigs crack like small bones,
and the frogs hear everything,
even the boy's breathing.

The frog swells.
The boy lengthens. He feels
the swollen throat, the woeful cries.
He has a cruel enemy
and no place to hide. To escape
the opaque pail he must leap
with light-tipped toes.

FLOWERS HAVE BEAUTY AND
ROOTS HAVE WORTH

Father sends me out to fetch you, but Mother, nothing
makes you want to come. Coatless and barefoot
you sit in the field more reliable than love.

Queen Anne's Lace and Blue Sailors,
stems filled with milky juice,
never molesting anyone, brush your arm.

You tell me the story of James James Morrison's
mother who drove to the end of town
in her golden gown and never returned, the story

of three foxes who didn't wear stockings
and kept their handkerchiefs in cardboard boxes.
I don't quite know where we are going, past evening
primrose,

its tangy fragrance, yarrow with yellow showy heads,
fireweed that follows on heels of carnage.
We could try to explain Father's seed

you opened wide for, that made me bloom
beside you in this field.
Blow a dandelion at its weediest.

The moon opens its mouth, lets out a light
like Father's flashlight.
Stones crown through the earth.

Here we are slumped over like cabbages.
Silver milkweed tricks the insects
until a whole podful of babies drifts off.

Who knows what will happen when a man
takes a woman's hand, when she touches his face,
when her body bends to his slapping?

SUNFLOWERS

Who could not love you
lifting blowzy, floppy heads higher than roses,
foxglove and daisy, making even a gray day golden.

Rising beside tomatoes, peppers, zucchini
equally sturdy, you spread saffron ruffles
and offer seeds without restraint.

Van Gogh knew what he was doing. Painting
with citron and ochre, he wrote to Theo,
The sunflower is mine in a way.
At his funeral, a kind of halo,
the gift of everlasting summer.

Rank, coarse, grown for fodder, horse banquet,
state flower of Kansas, home of twisters,
those old women bending over
looking for something to put in their pockets.

Made into bread and broth, oil, yellow dye,
cure for chest pain and snake bite,
you give leaves for bandages.
Eve may have loved you in Eden.

Hibernating in winter as hard black seed, a favorite
of birds, lifting up year after year, brazen, earthy, sturdy
as thistle, a bit uncouth, lion's mane yellow, gold tongue
thrust skyward and easily turned.

The season is short. In late summer sunflowers droop
thoughtful heads. We are not flowers or woman for long
but for this moment yellow blossoms follow the sun.

THE SEA LION

I decided to bring the sea lion home with us
in our Ford. His face lay on my brother's leg,
and he shed sand all over the back seat.
Father shouted, *What's all the racket back there?*
But he didn't turn around to look.

Back home, I hid the carcass, decomposing
and scummy, under dirty clothes in my bedroom.
He was a patient listener.
Clean up that room, my mother screamed.

That crumbling lump hid under the bed in the dorm at college,
then, already old, put on a blue ribbon for the wedding.
He became the best man.
Forsaking all others, till death us do part.

He is too big for the love seat. I stroke his ragged coat
and tell him about Mother, how they fixed her hair
before they cremated her, and about Father,
his hands like parchment in the coffin.
On Christmas morning he wears dark glasses
to hide his sunken eyes.

I put his picture in the family album.
Dull with dust, he dries out like Grandmother
in the nursing home, balding, fleshless,
asking what day it is, no longer watching
ghosts of leaves outside the window, fog.

The sea lion broods in the corner without a piano,
remembering summer, while he practices scales
on the wall. Memories of spiny fish, seaweed beckoning,
little ambushes of grief haunt his sleep.
Even the tide abandons us.

Finally his bones are pale as stars,
and I carry them back to the ocean.
Undertow takes him where rocks are beaten bare
and crows fly overhead, crying.

ASTIGMATISM

A wandering eye needs to be brought back like a bad cow.
I practiced looking cross-eyed, saw my nose
and doubled everything, read cards
through colors but couldn't deal a single image.
Ahead sat Mother in her chenille robe
working crosswords, eating Cheese-Its,
drinking gin. One eye rebelled like a shooting star
and went its own direction.

Look at me when I talk to you,
my father shouted,
and my eye wandered outside
to my sister twisting her hair and swinging.
When Father put his fist in my brother's ribs
my eye focused on the refrigerator door
keeping its secrets of cheese.
Ivy climbed out of a clay pot
and up the wall.

My pupils were startled.
When I asked my mother for advice
she said, *Look both ways.*
Don't let boys below the waist.
My eye carried my past in its dark. I wonder
if, when I sleep, it is still wandering.

I am not brave like the owl
who can stare unblinking into the night.
I am more the horse who kicks a wolf
without even turning her head.
Out of the corner of my eye I watch my husband
looking directly at the news. He moves away
from me, but I keep leaning in.

THE SCHOOL PHOTOGRAPHER

The photographer had a room like a box
where he controlled the light, kept prints all shades of grey
like Father's hair. In the morning he could make twilight,
in mid-day, midnight, shuttering stars,
reflectors, metal moons. He knew how to airbrush scars.

His wife sat under a blanket
in a wheelchair he pushed to football games,
wheels spindled silver.
I pictured lovemaking, saw him lift her
gently into bed where she lay calm, nude, immobile.

Did her soul glow
in the dark like an alarm clock?

My father walked past me to get to Mother.
Once she locked the door, and he broke it to splinters.
One night he pushed her downstairs.
Maybe he wanted her wheelchair-bound
but she lay in a heap, cried, then walked away.

One morning the photographer called me from class
for yearbook pictures. He said light following
his hand would be lovely on my hair.

I thought of my body passing through the lens
like a ghost, becoming one-dimensional,
kept forever on paper in the pose he shaped.
Then he asked me to lift my pleated skirt
from my saddle shoes so he could see
the angle of my legs.

Higher, he said, *lift it higher*
as he arranged the shadows.

He wasn't handsome, and I didn't like him
but thought of his wife in her wheelchair,
of Father when he broke down the door,
and I stood, letting him change the light.

MOTHER IN HEAVEN

Late one night when I could not sleep, I wondered
how Mother, who had trouble on earth,
would get along with angels,

linen wings ironed smooth and shaped just right
under chiffon, their voices on key at appointed hours.
Maybe she would not find it perfect in heaven.

Angels have chores. One had to rescue Daniel
and hold the south wind back. My mother, in her garden,
could only clip a gardenia to her idle hair.

Now, gazing down at the moon, she only pleases
or displeases God, and maybe looking down, gets dizzy,
as odd an angel as she was a mother.

Maybe, remembering her own rebellion, Vashti helps
when Mother stumbles, and maybe Rachel remembers
a daughter and a bride. Heaven has its own requirements.

If she is tipsy perhaps it won't matter. Clouds
can rinse her in holy water, the Milky Way shimmering
around her. I try to get on with my life.

Demons are another matter. Mother should be careful
whom she flutters up against.
The Devil himself can be charming

leading her into the kitchen
or hanging her by her ankles,
her shadow blue, smoke in her eyes.

POMEGRANATE

Along with citrus and peach
one of Buddha's three sacred fruits,
a gift from an old, poor woman.
He offered it to the demon Harti
and so cured her of eating children.
Some say each one holds 613 seeds
and each offers hope for a fruitful year.

At our house we cut them in quarters,
pulled back rinds exposing seeds in patterns,
possibly proof of the divine.
Juicy sacs in little pockets, translucent seeds
we pick out with our fingers,
rare jewels we crush between our teeth.

It is important to eat every seed
because one can't be sure
which came from Heaven.
Orchard of pomegranates Solomon sang of,
Persians painted them on their shields.
With saffron and mollusk shell
they helped dye Joseph's coat.

Their season is fleeting, but right when I need it.
I hold one in my hand and stroke
the deep-red rind, the calyx at the base.
One seed made Persephone
the bride of Hades.

This must have been Eve's apple,
sour sweet juice on her tongue,
all that knowledge, her mouth
the holy portal.

FOR MY OLDEST CHILD

I saw the angel in the marble
And I just chiseled til I set him free.
      —Michelangelo

To be a child again she will go back
past her own gray house, the yard with trees,
the table, oak chairs, the toaster,

past her child born before the wedding dress.
She will have to go past shoes used as weapons
to saltwater sandals and rubber boots

that know their way through the woods,
past the bed with rails
where she moaned, *The roses are lovely,*

but angels ruined my cake.
The maple drops red leaves in a language
only for children. The moon is a ripe banana.

She gives up the leather jacket
for the blue snowsuit with hood, its mittens safe
on strings. The fence is for pictures.

Gates, doors, windows let a child out,
let her in. A rag doll clearly has a heart,
but to get there she must walk past glass

her father broke with his fist, the belt
he used for beating. To find that holy child
she must put her heart in her pocket

and carry it like a wooly treasure
past the black sun to the crayoned yellow one
drawn over a house with a path and a brown cow.

A wolf is the dog who licks her face.
Every garden has secrets. Sunflowers bend
their heads to a child, and corn gives silk.

MY BROTHER ENTERS ENCHANTMENT

At dusk, deer emerge and graze on acorns,
twigs, and buds of viburnum and maple.
Like my brother in his younger days,

they don't bed down till dawn.
Rarely he thinks of those days in our father's store
when he set fire to Jim Adair's hat.

My brother rises from his chair by the fire,
puts on his blue sweater, walks away
from bluster and porch light.

 At first the deer stare at him from trees
along the river, grey brown coats and white patches
blending in with the birches, then they appear

from the foliage, one doe with twins
and several yearlings. My brother offers apples
carrots, lettuce, potato peeling, molasses,

then lays down the bowl and backs away.
Their large ears, supple movements, and wildness
entice him but he stands, quiet, calling to them

in whispers. They gaze at him with clear eyes
as they stand together in star silence,
as breath rises white in the cold air,

as the moon rises. Leaving hoofprints
like split hearts, the deer come closer
on jointy knees and graceful bodies and eat.

For this I am grateful,
my brother, with his good heart
in the low fog of twilight, feeding the deer.

ASHES TO ASHES

My sister wanted to last until the World Series
where the goal is reaching home.
She lived to watch Boston beat St. Louis in game one
but not game four when Boston won again.
She died at home, morphine a regular thing and visitors,
one with a black Tibetan bowl she stroked
into mournful song.

I wanted ritual, oil, rosewater, coins for the ferryman,
but two men carried her out
past leaves blowing across the lawn.

Five months later, the day after Ash Wednesday,
my brother followed her.
His wife put his ashes in a pot with roses.
Three children under an elder bush,
Ashes, ashes, all fall down.

At the beach my sister's husband holds out the box,
what is left of my sister, fine fragments of bone,
part of her foot, maybe, or clavicle.
A rule for scattering ashes, *keep your back to the wind.*
The cloud of her ash sails over the surf
leaving bone grit, death's gray residue in my hand.

And the sea takes her in its dark arms,
ashes like I scrape from the grill into a tin.
The extravagant ocean holds her along with graceful
moon jelly, winged kelp, and I want to follow
as if she went to sea in a beautiful pea green boat.

The Tibetan Book of the Dead says not to cry
because it confuses the dead and they cannot return.
Should anyone imagine finding on this beach

an answer, that person will hear constant banging
and clamor. At our feet, bird wings, violet crab claws,
limpets, little volcanos, sand, cold and wet,
our footprints erased by wave after wave
in their thunder and bluster.

In that margin of land, sea, and sky, a light film
of water shimmers in puddles
like a mirror with no face to hold.

LETTER FROM MY FATHER SOMEWHERE IN THE SOUTH PACIFIC, 1944

Dear Katherine,

I am mostly the same, but a long way out. I worry
you will think me different after the war.
Here, the dead become bad dreams. The ocean
could swallow all of us with a hiccup,
guns and all. Nights, I feel myself slip
through the weather. Days are hot,
and all we think about is home.

We just go on. Out here, alone,
we wash the ship and call it a woman. Rain falls
in sheets and drenches the scrubbed decks. We listen
to the ship and stare at the sea
for something moving.

If you know someone you don't like
send him to sea. I long to grow things,
vegetable stubbornness of tomato vines, to know only the garden
dying in the fall. I want to sail to you, remove your blouse,
shoes, lace underwear and slip past the sweet fragrance
of your skin. We could speak a code of moans
like the blues.

Water is pure and terrifying. Time folds
and your name melts on my tongue like chocolate.
The Japanese sure hold out. Guns, fighting
and death everywhere, town, farms, jungles and snow.

The sky empties itself on us. The earth turns
and the moon slithers like a silver fish.

Lena Horn is singing *St Louis Blues* on the radio.
If we were together, we could dance.

Love forever,
  Louis

POTATOES

From the wild wreck of my late summer garden
I fill a basket with potatoes, odd, misshapen,
earth apple, no two alike, regeneration from the roots up,
this stirring in the dark.

Wheat rises gold and becomes bread, for some,
the body of Christ, but potatoes arrive
with dirt on them, silent, and blind.

In Van Gogh's *Potato Eaters*, five figures
in yellow lamplight share a meal
around a worn table in the half dark shed,
as if those who ate potatoes
had joined them underground.

In the room laced with night, blue shadows,
light from their little lamp touches their bony hands,
their faces the color of unpeeled potatoes,
touches the women's dusty bonnets and the white cups
while one woman pours darkness from a small pot.

The potato's life is not without struggle either.
They battle leafhoppers, beetles, and blight
but roots find a way. The potato gives its eyes
for the next generation, two eyes for each new life.
Ancestors go back to the Incas.

From black soil, mottled lumps tumble out,
then my fingers plunge in, feeling for forms
cool and heavy in my hand, one like an ancient foot,
feeling the weight of the past.

Sliced, they give pale, damp rounds,
creamy moon flesh, milky white of gardenias,
cool, clean smell. By the end of summer vines lie slumped
over their hills and the sides of the bed, exhausted.

Van Gogh knew people who tilled the earth
with the same hands they put in the dish.
On the weathered table, the platter of potatoes,
fingers outstretched toward them.

Oh earth, arid or muddy,
mother of roots, tubers, insects, and worms,
you yield our food and, at the end,
cover us with your loamy quilt.

LEAVES GOING TO YELLOW

When the man squeezed the trigger
to make astonished feathers fly
he felt good. He gathered
in the birds by their sturdy legs
and held them for the picture,
gun in one hand, pheasants limp and bloody
in the other. The man liked the heft of gun
and bird, the words, *barrel, muzzle, trigger, grip.*

He liked to wear the mottled green and gold,
the creeping up behind,
shotgun holding steady
in his hand. He liked blending in with tree limbs
while marsh grass moved slightly
like morning, before the day enacts its amber.

Tall and thin, he could be handsome
but his eyes were cold. He knew
the blinds and shallows,
when northern birds are down
along the hunger lines, knew where to wait
and what to use. He liked to talk
about those ducks he was getting in a row.

When ground turns hard and distant apples drop,
corn is down, and pumpkins ripen for the candle,
the man put on his deathly green
and stalked through leaves, through our yard,
and through our house.

He loved his guns, once shooting
through the wall to our son's bedroom
to remind us who was boss.
He liked to put one on his lap to stroke

while he was drinking beer.
Houses fill with yellow light. Sky turns gray
and geese call each other home.

CURSE FOR AN EX HUSBAND

The style in those days was saddle shoes,
marry young, and follow his blue smoke:
now you may hit the bride.
The coffee table splintered
bleached oak under your feet and I grew pale.
In your hands, shoes were weapons as well as your
gun. I wish you a long life with your mother.
Be bald, both of you, and may your eyes
cloud over. She will live forever, forever beat
on the bathroom door. Stammer through breakfast.
Chew slowly, choke on remembering
something. Repeat old stories in each other's hairy ears.
May she be the only woman you hear moaning.
Get up from sleep each night and never find
what is missing. You'll live
but you won't feel like loving.
You fall to the floor but no one notices.
You look just like the linoleum.
Whack pears for light.
You are a frog that never changes.
Someone has your legs for supper. Memory will not
sleep, and you bury your father again
to keep from dreaming and wake up an old man,
the past circling your head like smoke.
Your mother is still watching. Each night you wet the bed,
and your neighbors look in and laugh.
Your dog goes off, and you jump straight up at the end
of his chain all day, waiting.
The moon slips away.
The children know the names of wildflowers
but forget yours.
The warmest thing you stroke is your gun.
Your shoes can't run.

COAT

Jacob made for Joseph a coat dyed with saffron,
pomegranate, mollusk shell,
and Joseph dreamed the sun, moon,
and eleven stars bowed down.
Still he was sold into slavery
and his father, inconsolable.

To my son I take wool with large, rugged buttons,
heavy socks, a sweater, and a blanket.
It is good to have a warm coat in winter, collar up
against wind swooping down the gorge,
rain getting colder, gray clouds close to the ground.

This coat is basic black, no need to dress
for the dark that comes surely as winter. My son lives
in a world of shadows, a long way from snowsuit
and cowboy quilt.
Bless this warm coat.
Bless this soup and bread,
and may he rise as many times as it takes
to find his good heart.

Birches have dropped yellow leaves, and winter
brings bitter red berries and long nights.
We talk of cold, the food, his need for shoes.
Some say, *Here comes a dreamer. Cast him into the wilderness
and give him no water.*
If I rend my own clothes could we be comforted?

I give my son this black pea coat.
May it resist wind and rain
even when the moon holds a hand to her face

and angels disappear like lights going out in windows.
If he loses everything, again,
I will bring food, shoes, a blanket and a warm coat.

THE HEART HOLDS OUT EMPTY HANDS

By December my daughter slumps back to my house
with a bag of clothes, a box of noodles,
and a few spices, her back so thin her spine makes buttons
down her cotton shirt. Her legs barely carry her
upstairs. Hands drift, lost in her hair. Only her diamond
intact.

The mouth, full of a man, forgets
the tongue is also for tasting apples, oatmeal
with cream and cinnamon. She yearns
for sleep, the long swoon, and hordes cans of soup
and boxes of crackers in the closet with her shoes.
In her pocket a squashed cookie wrapped in a napkin,
a little something for grief.

I don't even have a coffee pot, she says.
It's hard to decide what to wear
with three voices in my head.

One voice says, *The blue dress is lovely,*
but the voice of her father says, *She looks like a whore,*
and the man with his hand over her mouth says,
Cut off your hair.
I say, *Remember dark chocolate, almonds, papaya.*

If I am going to eat, she says, I want it fiery,
I want to feel it burn. I want to taste Tabasco,
red hot peppers that make me break a sweat.

Even the bath runs hot as she can stand. Heat
from every pore. A fever left to run its course.
When the flavor's gone from life, she tries to make it up
with five-star curries. Night descends. My daughter lights
candles to purify the air, fasts, and waits for a vision.

LET YOURSELF CHANGE SHAPE

My father loved fishing.
Wearing waders around the yard
he cast hooks into tomatoes for practice.

He taught me to cook in cast iron.
Cleaning fish means gutting
everything that makes them alive.

I tried to be a fish, flopping
on smooth stones in the sun
but my father knew what he wanted.

The evil fairy cackled,
You are an ordinary girl
whose father loves only fish.

My father has followed his sinking line
and I spend hours in the aquarium
learning colors and feeding habits,

the water music, how salmon
make the long swim back.
When the moon rises, my spine curves

and I dream cool skin, layer after layer
of silver. Cold and slippery, I practice
bending in the middle. I am afraid

I will become a goose, duck, pig,
or cow and not a flashing knife blade in water.
Glittering with salt, I have sensitive feelers,

sharp bones. My father walks farther
into the ocean, blind breakers slapping his thighs
everything wet and shining,

his line slicing the sky
searching for the perfect arc.
My hook enters his heart.

TRYING TO CHANGE MY LIFE WITH CANARD À L'ORANGE

Sauce, most important, rich, meaty duck essence,
flavored with orange peel and Madeira,
pleasant orange flavor, not too sweet, fragrance of citrus.

The whole meal a two-day project, but my family was worth
it, I thought. Oh Julia, you change the lives of so many,
couldn't you change mine?

Nothing should interfere with flavors of the duck.
I take out the wishbone and wish. My black dog
stares at the oven the way he stares at the ducks in the park.

I love the earthy fragrance of his paws.
Fall drifts toward cold and dark, leaves losing their grip
on trees, and I am losing mine.

My daughter, my restless angel, grows tired of all the beds,
the men, and empties her glass of wine over and over,
her shoulder blades failed wings.

My son, my beautiful boy, wears his red baseball cap
backwards, *Mom* tattooed on his chest. A snake writhes
along the arm he scratches with his knife.

My husband does not take his eyes from TV—
some football game—wins and losses. My stepson
grabs the duck, browning beautifully, from the oven,

because he thinks it is his dead sister. He cries for his mother
who left him, puts his cockapoo in the microwave and laughs.
Every woman should have a blowtorch, said Julia.

Be fearless and have fun.
My husband does not get up from his chair.
But back to the duck, back in the oven and weeping.

Careful cooking is love, said Julia, and I believe
in gathering at the table, bread and wine, an offering,
but we are on orange alert.

TULIPS

It was January when I bought them
from the flower lady's stand
on Eastlake Avenue and carried them two miles
home. My hands almost froze. At first
the tulips were tight-lipped, five in a bunch.
I cut their stems and put them in an earthenware jar
in front of the window on a wicker chest.

Each one had six overlapping petals, bright red
with ruffled edges pulled tight as a turban.
When you arrived, late afternoon light
warmed each rosy lip.
Long stems bending, heads turned
a mosaic of broken color
bright enough to advertise.

A long tongue could reach down
to the yellow light of the stamen. Our lips
followed softness, the good taste of mouth.
The next day, hungry
for different scenes, we left them
and took a ferry out to a lighthouse
flashing in fog.

We could barely see land,
or lights blinking from houses.
Black and white cows with soft faces
grazed behind fences the color of pewter.
We could have been anyone.
Inside, tulips opened their mouths. Petals flushed
and dropped everything beside the jar.

SEPTEMBER, ROGUE RIVER

In the time of sun growing more distant, blackberries,
more thorns than berries, blue sailors,
Queen Anne's lace lining the path to the river blinking silver

through trees, umber and burnt-orange, my father died,
many years ago, two husbands, both my children
now also dead. How exacting death is.

I can almost see his face in the water, hair barely gray,
like submerged stones,
those stones he walked over in his waders

casting his line in a long arc over ripples.
The rod trembled in his hand
before it lifted line, leader, and fly

off the surface, gave them a good toss
over his head, toward heaven,
and shot them forward

so they landed in the water without a splash,
each cast an effort to make a fresh start in life.
Trout come by grace, and my father

found grace in cold water when he held that rod,
a fly at the end he tied
while sitting on his bed

in the small bedroom down the hall from Mother.
Rocks rose where the river shook itself with spray
then fell back into curves, green and gray bubbled light,

speckles from pine and fir, water going from roar to whisper.
He tried to make fishing a world perfect and apart,
a world with rainbows and hard fighting steelhead.

Having a hook pierce its lips or jaw is painful
for a fish. If they survive, they remember being caught
for a year. Fish want to live.

Males lie side by side with females to breed.
In that same river, a whirlpool spun Shirley Telfer
down where a rock held her long black hair

until she grew loose and her body let go
of heat. One of my students, a golden boy, swimming
on a hot summer day, cramped and went under.

Instead of light and air, silence
and all goes black, like it did for my father
on the white island of his hospital bed.

Today, those good parents, blue and black Steller's jays,
gregarious and talkative, watch and fly from branch
to contorted branch of madrone. What do birds think of us?

Still I hear my father's voice. I wanted him to talk
to me, wanted him to say, "*Do not marry that man.
He is nothing but trouble.*"

BEGONIA

She is better off now, said Scottie Trumbly
when she brought a yellow begonia after my mother died,
but I did not believe her.

The begonia was lovely though, draped over its pot
like my mother lay draped over her bed,
arms trailing toward the floor where one day she lay

bleeding. Esophageal rupture, they called it,
often occurring in alcoholics. For years her skin turned yellow
but not as bright as the dusting of buttercups

or the begonia's showy flowers. I loved the begonia,
maybe too much, as I watered, fertilized, gave it just enough sun
so it kept blooming all summer, even as leaves turned ochre

and nights turned colder, until the first frost
when it began to remove its light, like my mother did
when I needed her, needed a guide for the dark woods

and could not decide: Red sweater or blue?
Short hair or long? What about bangs?
Should I eat something that has a mother?

How to deal with Bobby Harrell when he dips
my braids in the inkwell? Is there a heaven?
Will we go there? What about Father?

I kept learning tubers, small brown bowls, sensitive to cold.
Hairy nests protect sprouts and buds in the moist earth.
Such beauty does not make grief easier,

but still my hands dig for some elusive answer.
Dark comes early, then summer ends and the dying
turn yellow. A few birds continue their song.

DRAGONFLIES

The ocean slaps and drums. Starfish, red
and ochre, and colorful anemones wave all directions
like children, smells of saltwater and kelp.

Wild burnished flight, a cloud
of gauzy dragonflies fluttery as dreams,
little flying matchsticks,

they rise from the marsh
and climb into air.
Almost invisible in shadow,

they easily find one another.
At the end of her slender abdomen one spot
lights like a lamp for her mate.

What iridescent bodies, blue frenzy.
My black dog lopes along by my side
then begins muscular leaps, high turns,

head lifted. The dragonfly misses nothing
and eats in flight like she mates,
while the earth turns under her.

WATER, CUP, SPOON, HOUSE

In the dark sky of his mind, my husband is back
on a ship headed for China during WWII. He is seventeen.
During a typhoon, that whirlwind of water, waves wash over
the ship, fury at sea.

As rain smacks our bedroom window with little fists,
he slides one long leg out of the covers.
    The water is up to my knees, he says,
    We are going to drown.

Each day grows dark earlier.
Flesh disappears from his good bones,
and his head sinks lower on the pillow.

We should be used to autumn, cattail fur,
frost, geese rising on wings, gone,
but we console ourselves, they will return.

Memory falls in great chunks, forty years gone, fifty,
me with them.

    Where are we? he asks.
    Why are we here?
    How did we get here?

Those old questions.
He forgets his own need for food and cannot name
what he is losing. A spoon becomes his hand,
lifting and lowering, circling the cup,
even as his mind circles the cup for the word.

Tao Te Ching says, *What makes the vase is where it is not.*

I fell into my coffee, my husband says,
When do we go home?

Nights grow colder. Birds leave. No answer
for anything. Crows speak in tongues,
everything off key.

When do those men come to get me? he asks.
Does this house travel? Does this bed travel?

My husband keeps saying the same thing, trying
to get it right, to get the right answer,
the song we all sing.
He wanders and gets lost in our house.

Don't go without me, he begs,

and will not let go of my arm.

He leaves on a journey to a place
where he does not speak the language.

Who are you? he asks,
Are you married?
Where do you live?

He is leaving home, leaving his comfortable chair,
the familiar kitchen table, his favorite blue cup,
our bed, his fur slippers.

Sing to me, he says.
I can't sleep

with all those people
looking in the window.
Something is not right.

He is back on the farm as a boy
and his father is slaughtering
the calf he raised, the calf he loved.
He refuses to shower.

    I could drown, he says.

He reaches and touches our dog who licks his hand
and rubs his muzzle on his knee.

    I am shimmering like a limb.
    The railroad doesn't go there, he says,

from his traveling bed.
So this ends, with tears and a journey.

CROW

Like dark angels they strut and flutter,
shapes far back in the brain
digging beneath the surface
like memory,
take us to the bare bones of things.
Good brains, glistening feathers
in the gray sky, in trees, on the ground,
everywhere, like grief,
sharp caws, the first thing I hear in the morning.
If messenger from the gods,
what message?
Wingtip feathers, spread like fingers,
row against sky
at once in love with both sides
of the moon.
Crows smear themselves with crushed ant oil,
memorize human faces,
and sing softly to attract mates.
Twice the size of a blue jay
they mull over found pennies and buttons,
eat almost everything,
earthworms, old sandwiches, dead seagulls.
Always someplace ahead,
fierce even in silence.
Razzle dazzle flying
trips me up, pulls me down.
Van Gogh painted a wheatfield,
a path going nowhere,
a turbulent sky crazed with crows
who see everything and know transformation.
Crow leaves tracks on my face,
three toes pointed forward,
one long one back.
Under the shadow of his wing

he is the world with my eyes closed.
When stars go out
he has the last word.

FISH IN THE BLOOD AND
A BIRD WATCHING

Police took your body in its traveling clothes
to the morgue, then the funeral home
where they washed your hair

in fire. From the swamp of my body,
Pisces child, fists curled, you swam
into this fallen world,

child with curls and a woman with my eyes
and my bones. You could not sleep,
like fish, could not close your eyes.

Somebody saw you Thursday and said you were fine
then, that hot August Saturday,
death climbed in the window

and found you alone in your room
where you fell like a child,
surrounded by dust motes like stars.

So much for the sparrow.
You quit singing, ate nothing but smoke.
Nothing can stop the end

when it decides to come
like water churning, someone going under.
Your heart stopped and you became fire and air.

Ash inadequate for a body.
When I go where you are, my hope
is the first words I hear will be, *Hi Mom*.

Green hovers over your grave, a veil
between one world and another.
I take roses and poppy seeds to feed the dead,

who return disguised as birds.
Oh Honey, come back,
eat your dinner.

THE BURIAL OF CASAGEMAS

after the painting by Picasso, 1901

Death and ascension, the body, mourners, blue
of the Egyptian underworld, two women, nude

except for stockings, blue on one, the only red
the stockings of another. A woman, alone,

wrapped in a black shawl bends over the body
covered in a white shroud.

I am that woman. When my son
lay in the viewing room of Riverside Abbey,

I took white roses, lavender, and a letter.
I know the dead do not stay warm but was shocked

by his cold hand and cheek, his body once muscle
and bristle. Mine the only breath.

Nothing to break the silence but my own voice
saying goodbye to my only son

who lay wrapped in a white blanket,
hands crossed over his chest

as if he were flying into himself.
For his ascension, Casagemas sits on a white horse,

arms outstretched. A woman kisses him.
My son, alone in his room, lying on a single cot,

may have looked at his small lamp, his cup, his glass,
his book and wondered, *why not.*

Maybe when he put that needle in his arm, he saw angels
who offered caresses with feathers of their great wings.

Maybe he laid his head
on an angel's breast and heard her music.

BLUE HERON

She is the blue distance
of everything we kiss,
the guttural cry of departure.
How can any of us protect ourselves?
My husband turns from me,
and the dead slip in.
The heron is bent
like an old woman.
She is a solitary feeder
and I am afraid
my very presence drives her away,
but I return often
when she isn't there,
my black dog by my side,
watching changes of light
on water. I look for blue
on the edge, the promise
of plumage. When I least
expect it, the heron appears,
still as wood pilings.
She knows how to avoid
storms and how to be alone,
staying in shallow margins,
waiting. The air is cold
as earth. My body kisses the blue.

TURNING THE BONES

Sometimes you woke from your silence, took my hand
from where it was chopping vegetables and pulled me close
for a dance. *Mood Indigo* taught us blues,

my feet shadowing yours,
your arm around my waist, my arm on your shoulder,
that last long kiss, your fragrance of lilac and orange.

We hug and sway with the music
like any teenagers.
That muted horn touches everything.

Bluer than blue can be.
Our shadows know the dark and still they have a song,
all of me, why not take all of me.

We held on a long time while you still had flesh
to touch and hold, before that long good bye,
parts of your memory slipping away,

before you forgot who I am, before grass
closed over your grave. When elephants mourn
their dead they touch the body

with their feet and fondle the bones with their trunk.
Dolphins nudge and push the carcass of their dead.
When my children died, they were taken away,

but a chimpanzee mother carries the body of her dead child
around for days. The dead can return to us in many ways.
In Madagascar, every seven years tribes dig up their dead,

clean them and dress them in silks for a party
before they are returned to the crypt. They talk
to their dead, tell them the latest news

and ask for guidance. When you return to me
in the kitchen I run my fingers along your bones
and your dust, feel your sternum close to mine,

the beautiful spiral of radius and ulna and 27 bones
of your hand around my waist. A tenor sax can touch
on old miseries and can turn even the oldest bones

from a time to mourn to a time to dance.
I keep my good black dress, keep your shirts
like white sails on their wooden hangers,

your polished shoes holding your ghost feet.
Sometimes I take your Harris tweed jacket,
charcoal and blue and hold it

where your shoulder would be, feel the texture
of wool, lift my hand
to where you used to hold it and move my bare feet

in those old, slow rhythms.
For your funeral a man played *Over the Rainbow*
on the cello, and we could have danced.

INVISIBLE CHOIR

Sometimes the long slow rain seems never to end.
Leaves lap it up, and I head for the pond
where I hear my own footsteps, spatter of drops
on trees, and creaking calls of frogs.
Here, close to the city, they live
a secretive life, neighbors we know by their song.
If we get too close, they grow quiet.

Life is fragile even with a golden ball, a magic ring,
and a princess. So much dying.
A tadpole must deal with water beetles
and fish. Adults evade bats, snakes,
men building houses and malls. Everywhere
poison. They could teach me shades of green,
hiding and changing.

Tonight the air vibrates with lusty hums, grunts,
and peeps, melodious as birds' trill,
calls for a mate. Each male has his own
distinct call and jumps
for the joy of mating.

Who wouldn't love green gold jewels?
If a frog came courting to my house
I would kiss him with wet lips
and raspberry tongue
for his smell of damp moss and fern,
his voice like a fat cello.

PEONY

Early spring and my friend announces a stirring
among the peonies, small red tinged shoots.

Grown from a tuber, a survivor, their history goes back
thousands of years. Native to China.

State flower of Indiana. Tight green bulbs
swell and unfurl, petals changing color,

sensual as any woman, with fragrance of rose,
honey, citrus, and musk, smallest petal

embraced by the largest, multilayered
like pompoms. Decorative stamens

thrill like the gold of sunflowers and goldfinch,
a party in the middle, mauve at the shaggy center.

Big as a fist, heart on the sleeve, shirt off,
modesty gone, come hither look, more sex than violence.

I no longer have an other in my bed
who nurtures, so I look to earthy beds

where plants grow root to root and what falls—
limbs, petals, leaves, and birds,

makes more earth, where my mother, father,
sister, brother, husband, daughter, and son

lie tucked in the dark, where I take flowers,
talk to the dead and shake my fist at the sky.

Hemlock and fir hover over their names and dates.
Life is not perfect for peonies, either.

Botrytis and powdery mildew can do serious damage.
Bronze beetles feed on peony blossom

until they are drugged by lust. Ants love
the sweet nectar of buds. Peonies hate to be moved.

Relative of the sunny buttercup,
big, busty, cheerful mound of ruffles

like a 50s prom dress, blooms, silky as a negligee,
so heavy they dip, bend, sometimes topple and break,

sad flounces scattering on the dirt path. Some think
the peony an emanation from the moon,

protecting houses near which it grows. Tousled,
blowzy, I sleep in half a bed. The dead return

at night and sometimes morning and afternoon.
The peony sheds its own light. In June, my friend

offers a bright pink, sweet-scented blossom,
and I take it, pink light of solace splashing our hands.

ABOUT THE AUTHOR

Victoria Wyttenberg likes to quote Richard Hugo from his book, *The Triggering Town*, that "The poem is always in your hometown, but you have a better chance of finding it in another." Wyttenberg's hometown is Grants Pass, in Southern Oregon, and her obsessions go back to her growing up there, often to family issues and to feeling solace from nature, the Rogue and Applegate Rivers, the hot summer sun, the smell of rain.

She taught English at the High School level for thirty years, four years at Grants Pass High School and twenty six years at Sunset High School, Beaverton, Oregon. She continued taking classes at Portland State University and Reed College, took a developmental leave and attended the University of Washington as a graduate student, then returned to full time teaching and completed the work for her Masters of Fine Arts in Creative Writing, Poetry. Wyttenberg won the Richard

Hugo Prize from *Poetry Northwest* and the Academy of American Poets Prize at the University of Washington.

When she retired from full-time teaching, she taught part-time for several years, and has continued taking classes in writing and art. Since her husband and both of her children have died, many of her poems deal with grief and the effort to find comfort in the natural world. She lives in Portland, Oregon with her dog.